Catholicus

# The Doctrine of Justification

and the harmony of the Apostles Paul and James considered - with

particular reference to the treatise of Bishop O'Brien - in three letters,

reprinted from the British Magazine, designed for the use of students in

divinity

Catholicus

**The Doctrine of Justification**
*and the harmony of the Apostles Paul and James considered - with particular reference to the treatise of Bishop O'Brien - in three letters, reprinted from the British Magazine, designed for the use of students in divinity*

ISBN/EAN: 9783337252571

Printed in Europe, USA, Canada, Australia, Japan

Cover: Foto ©Lupo / pixelio.de

More available books at **www.hansebooks.com**

THE

# DOCTRINE OF JUSTIFICATION

AND THE

HARMONY OF THE APOSTLES

## Paul and James

CONSIDERED,

WITH PARTICULAR REFERENCE TO THE TREATISE OF
BISHOP O'BRIEN.

IN THREE LETTERS,

REPRINTED FROM THE BRITISH MAGAZINE.

---

DESIGNED FOR THE USE OF STUDENTS IN DIVINITY.

---

LONDON:

RIVINGTONS, WATERLOO PLACE.

1862.

# LETTER I.

Sir,

The doctrine of justification is one to which, though already the theme of so much wearisome, angry, and often verbal controversy, we may be excused for reverting again and again, if it is with any hope of correcting error, or reconciling differences. I venture, accordingly, at a season of the year when perhaps the demands on your valuable space are least oppressive, to ask a share of it, for the proofs, or what appear to me to be the proofs, of the three following propositions. 1. That justification is from first to last, by faith, and by faith only. 2. That there is nothing in this doctrine militating with the principle, as asserted by St. James, that "a man is justified by works, and not by faith only," according to the plainest and most obvious sense of those expressions. 3. That St. James's expressions will not admit of any other meaning, or, in other words, that the meaning of St. James's language, (which alone has given rise to the notion of a discrepancy between his doctrine

A 2

of justification and the doctrine of St. Paul,) is, notwithstanding, the true meaning.

On the establishment of the first of these three propositions I shall not feel it necessary to bestow any large amount of labour. My concern is chiefly with the second of them. I will remark, however, that I yield to no one in the sense which I entertain of the importance of the doctrine. I subscribe *ex animo* to the sentiment of its being " articulus stantis vel cadentis ecclesiæ." In this doctrine, according to the just remark of Bishop O'Brien (Sermon 4), is involved the notion of the Gospel as "a scheme of free forgiveness." Therefore, it "is of faith that it might be by grace." Mingle any " work or deserving " on the part of man with the grace which it proposes, and its salvation no longer is gratuitous. It is only so far forth, as it is *of* faith, that it is *by* grace, and admit, in consequence, that the salvation is *entirely* by grace, and it will follow, that it is also *entirely* "of faith," that we are justified by faith, and by faith *only*, justified from first to last in the character and capacity of "ungodly" without any thing " whereof to glory," or any occasion afforded to us for "despising others," for saying, "Stand by thyself, I am holier than thou," to the worst or most obdurate of the species. Is there, then, 2ndly, any thing in such a doctrine inconsistent with St. James's principle, that "a man is justified by works, and not by faith only," in the simplest and most natural sense of the expressions? It is imagined to be obvious that there is. But is it, then, (let me ask,) inconsistent to suppose that, in the case of the woman with the issue of blood, her "*faith* had saved her," and at the same time that she "*touched* the border" of the Saviour's garment, and that "*immediately* she was healed?" Is it inconsistent to suppose that "by *faith* the Israelites passed through the sea, as by dry land," and yet, that they crossed it *on their feet?* Was it *partly*, again, by faith, and *partly* by works, that David overcame Goliath, because, although he tells him that he came against him "in the name of the Lord," he employed, notwithstanding, the instrumentality of a sling and a stone, and a certain acquired dexterity in using them, for accomplishing his overthrow? We allege, perhaps, nothing of this kind; we admit that it was "her faith," and her faith *only*, which "healed" the woman with the issue of blood; and their faith, and their *faith only*, which carried the Israelites through the Red Sea, as on dry ground; and the name of the Lord, and this *only*, in which David went against Goliath, though in all these instances a certain "work" concurred and was instrumental in producing the result; and where, then, is the inconsistency in affirming at once that we are justified by faith, and by faith only; and affirming at the same time, (in the easiest and most natural sense of the expressions,) that "a man is justified by works, and not by faith only?" To be justified, indeed, "by the deeds of the law," and to be justified "by faith" are opposite and contradictory conditions; but to be justified "by faith," and "by" the "works" *which are faith operating and coming out into display*, is precisely the same thing. Who ever heard, indeed, in other instances, of an opposition and rivalry between a moral principle and the course of action which results from it? Is it, for instance, in derogation of the patriotism, the gallantry, or other qualities displayed in the performance of them, that his brilliant or self-sacrificing achievements are enumerated in the hearing of some benefactor of his country, and that he is told that the honours and rewards which she bestows upon him have been *earned by those achievements?* Is it not, on the contrary, precisely as *manifestative of the qualities* which they are considered as displaying, that those achievements are so praiseworthy? Is it not precisely the *qualities* which are praised *in* the achievements—achievements which have not a particle of moral worth—have not the smallest character of *laudableness* whatever, beyond that which they derive from the patriotic self-devotion, the personal gallantry, the military skill, the statesmanship, as it may be, which is seen, or supposed to be inscribed on them? The achievements are not something *added* to, and thus capable of coming into competition with the principles of character which led to the performance of them; they *are*, on the contrary, those *principles in manifestation*, and (for any moral value that attaches to them) they are *nothing else*.

And where, then, is the contradiction, when we affirm, on the one hand, that we are justified by faith, and by faith only; and on the other, that "a man is justified by works, and not by faith only?" It is, however, possibly inquired at this point, what it is that we then mean by faith, and by faith *only?* The reply may be given in the words of Hooker, " To the imputation of Christ's death for remission of sins we teach faith *alone* necessary, wherein it is not our meaning to separate thereby faith from any other quality or duty which God requireth to be matched therewith, but from faith to seclude, in justification, the fellowship *of worth through precedent works, as the Apostle Paul doth* [1]." Or the reply may be given in the very similar words of St. Augustine; for St. Paul's doctrine (St. Augustine says) is, " ut nemo meritis *priorum* operum *arbitretur* se pervenisse ad donum justificationis quæ est in fide. In hoc enim se Gentibus in Christo credentibus Judæi præferre cupiebant quod dicebant se meritis bonorum operum quæ in lege sunt ad evangelicam gratiam pervenisse ideoque scandalizabantur multi qui ex eis crediderant quod incircumcisis Gentibus Christi gratia tenderetur, unde Ap. Paulus dicit posse hominem sine operibus, sed *præcedentibus,* justificari per fidem. . . . *Quapropter* non sunt sibi contrarii Apostoli Paulus et Jacobus, quia ille dicit de operibus quæ *fidem præcedunt,* iste de iis quæ

---

[1] Answer to Christian Letter, Keble's edit. vol. ii. p. 701.

fidem sequuntur; sicut etiam ipse Paulus multis
locis ostendit [2]."

I proceed to the third of the three propositions
which I hoped to be able to establish—the proposition, namely, that St. James's language admits
of no other than the meaning which has given
rise to the notion of a discrepancy between his
doctrine of justification and the doctrine of St.
Paul. And the proof of this proposition I might
safely perhaps leave to the united testimonies of
Hooker and Augustine just recited. It would,
again, appear to have sufficient proof in the consideration, that this is certainly the simplest and
most natural sense to assign to his expressions,
and the one, accordingly, the authority and claims
of which result, at once, in their full force, directly
that the reason for diverting them to a different
and less natural signification is seen to be devoid
of any real foundation.

But, lastly, this meaning of St. James's language may be argued from the difficulty in which
controversialists have found themselves involved
in seeking any other for it. Dr. Owen, for instance, and a host of writers of his school, interpret it one way: Dr. Wardlaw and his disciples
are "dissatisfied" with this interpretation, and
interpret it another. Bishop O'Brien deviates
from both. On *his* principles, the Apostle's language *has* the meaning for which we are contend-

---

[2] Lib. de Diversis Quæstionibus, tom. vi. p. 67.

ing, only (according to the Bishop) he *is not seri-ous in what he says.* His meaning is not really
what his words express. He affirms, indeed, that
a man *in foro Dei* is "justified by works, and not
by faith only," but he does not mean what he
says. I accept the authority of the Bishop as
conclusive, with regard to the force of the expressions, and this might, under the circumstances,
seem sufficient; for the Bishop would probably
be the first to admit the meaning which he claims
for them to be uncalled for and inadmissible, ex-
cept upon the supposition, that the contrary interpretation goes to put St. James at doctrinal
variance with St. Paul. And as I have shown, as
I hope, that this supposition is mistaken, it may
seem needless to expose the error of the Bishop's
interpretation. Can any thing, at the same time, be
more evident, according even to the Bishop's own
showing, than that the Apostle's entire argument
turns upon the point, that faith is valueless *merely*
as *faith*, and apart from certain moral and practical results in which it issues? "What doth it
profit, though a man say he hath faith, and *have
not works?* Can faith (or *his* or *this* faith, as the
Bishop) save him?" The argument does not turn
on his *saying* that he has faith, when he has nothing of the kind, but upon his *wanting works.*
What does it "profit *if* (ἐὰν) a man—have not
works?" His either *saying* he has faith, or actually having it, would make no difference. It is
the absence of works, that the Apostle fastens on.

And so again—"If a brother or sister be naked or destitute of daily food, and one of you say to them, Depart in peace, be ye warmed and filled, notwithstanding that ye give them not, &c., what doth it profit?" As much as to say, a man is no more to be justified by faith without works, than the hungry or the naked are to be warmed and nourished, without food or clothing, by good wishes or fair words. Again—"You have faith. Well, but it is not faith *as* faith, which is of any value, for the devils also believe and tremble. Wilt thou know, O vain man, that faith *without works* is dead, being *alone?* And thus was not Abraham our father justified by works, when he offered up Isaac his son upon the altar?" "By doing so he showed that he *feared* God." He showed that the "faith" which had previously been "imputed unto him for righteousness," was out and out obedience in principle and germ, and that he was justified by it *in this view of it.* And what, accordingly, justified Rahab the harlot? Not an opinion or profession, but a service which she did the Israelites, expressive, indeed, of the fact that she believed that God was with them of a truth, but apart from which this faith, ineffectual and inoperative, would have been of no benefit to her in the world. I think it, then, evident, from the entire train of the Apostle's reasoning, that his "conclusion," that "a man is justified by works, and not by faith only," is perfectly serious and formal. He means that while a penitent is justi-

fied by faith, as "the obedience," in "order" to
which "the Gospel is preached among all na-
tions," so he is justified by works, as the same
obedience in its progress and developement, in ac-
cordance with that remark of Field's, "But some
man may perhaps say, that a thing that was due
in respect of the habit resting in the mind may
become due in respect of the act done; and, con-
sequently, that that which was due one way may
become more ways due. Surely we make no question but it may, because it was due to the habit as
to the root of such an action, when occasion should
be offered and opportunity serve, and not other-
wise ³."

It is true, then, that works are justifying only
as they spring from, and thus express the opera-
tion of, a principle of *faith in divine mercy;* but
then, again, this faith itself is only justifying as
it receives Christ, as much in one as in another
of His offices, as much submitting the believer's
mind to His illumination and instructions as his
Prophet, and the believer's heart and life to His
government and regulation as his King, as de-
pending for pardon and acceptance upon Him as
his Priest—the believer confiding in God's grace,
not separately as exercised in the justification of
his person, but jointly, as exercised also in the sanctification of his soul; not expecting his happiness
merely from exemption from sin's punishment,

³ Book v. c. 20.

but, along with this, from deliverance also from its power; not merely from a title obtained to the rewards of righteousness, but, as well, from a capacity obtained at the same time to bring forth those "fruits of righteousness which are by Jesus Christ to the glory and the praise of God." How true and striking that remark of Richard Baxter [4], "Some may think that the high things required in the Gospel, self-denial, forsaking all, &c., are *more than the mere receiving a free gift.* But .... on consideration, it will all appear to be *no more* materially, for, 1st, When we say that it is the receiving the free gift, we must mean—*according to the nature and use of that gift*—as if you be required to take food, the meaning is, to eat it, and not to throw it away. If you be required to take such a man to be your king, master, tutor, husband, physician, &c.—the meaning is, *as such*, to the *use of his proper* office. And so, to accept of God as *God*, that is, as our absolute ruler, owner, and end, and Christ as our Saviour, prophet, priest, and king, and the Holy Ghost as our sanctifier, to illuminate, quicken, and renew us, is the sum of all the positives of the Gospel. 2ndly, For this very acceptance of them in this nature and to this use, *includeth the using of them* after *accordingly*, and if we *do not so use them, we thereby reject* them, and lose our own benefit of them, as he that eateth not his meat, and he that

---

[4] Catholic Theology, part ii. sect. 10.

weareth not his clothes, and he that learneth not of his teacher." So entirely does Richard Baxter differ from the sentiment [5], that " to include obedience in the nature of faith is to deviate manifestly from its meaning in common language." So little does he justify the Bishop in " presuming" that this is a sentiment, the truth of which, " all who contend for this, as its scriptural sense, would be ready to acknowledge." On the contrary, after reconciling the Apostles Paul and James on principles (if I understand him correctly) substantially identical with those asserted in this paper, he concludes with saying, " All this justification by works St. James is for, and it is *undeniable by any thing but prejudice, ignorance, and siding-peevishness* [6]." I should feel ashamed, myself, to resolve into no better principles the theology of so many great divines ; but this is the sentiment of Richard Baxter; and I wish (I own) that Richard Baxter's sentiments and reasonings on this subject were more known and more considered than I am apprehensive that they are.

I am, sir, your obedient servant,

CATHOLICUS.

[5] O'Brien, Serm. i. p. 9.
[6] Cath. Theol. part ii. sect. 26, ad fin.

# LETTER II.

SIR,

The doctrine of justification by faith is one of that fundamental importance, that every over-statement of the doctrine tending to impair its simplicity or embarrass its proof, is to be deprecated as a serious injury to the interests of pure and undefiled religion. This injury, I fear, has but too frequently been done. The inquirer after truth has been perplexed and, probably, misled. The formalist has been confirmed in his disastrous error by the title given to him to identify his cause with that of justification by works, as asserted by St. James. Against numbers struggling, perhaps, practically, for all that is spiritual and vital in Christianity, it has operated still as a legitimate and merited prejudice, that they have stood forward, at the same time, as the advocates of a theology, doctrinally absurd and antinomian, opposed to the plainest statements of the Word of God, and unknown in the Church Catholic (according to the confession or avowal of one of the most devoted patrons of this doctrine) for fourteen, at least, out of the first fifteen hundred years of Christianity. The Romanist has found a signal triumph in the prevalence, among Protestants, of an error in the opposite extreme, more transparent, if not more malignant, than his own. The controversy has been put upon the issue of the Protestant's ability to evince a doctrine to be at once unscriptural and unspiritual, which is asserted in terms by the Apostle James. He has identified the cause of Protestantism with a theology which sets Scripture, tradition, and reason at defiance. It is no slight evidence of the grossness of papal error, that Protestantism should have been able to hold its ground under the pressure of so serious a disadvantage. It is no trifling token of the tenacity of life of the doctrine of justification by faith, that it should have at all survived the wounds which have been thus inflicted upon it in the house of its friends. How important, at the same time, that a doctrine so " wholesome," and so " very full of comfort," should neither be perverted nor disguised. I have ventured, in a former paper, to furnish what I conceive to be the scriptural and rational account of the relations of faith and works. I am desirous, in a second contribution, to add what I can of confirmation to my previous argument, by considering one or another of the principal objections, commonly relied upon, against the scheme which I am advocating.

One of these, and the one to which I shall con-

fine myself on this occasion, is, that the Apostle
Paul excludes *all* works, and not some works only,
from the office of justifying; and thus, among
others, the works by which, according to St.
James, " a man is justified, and not by faith only."
That the contrary of this is the sentiment at once
of Hooker and Augustine, we have seen already in
my paper of last month. According to each of
these authorities, the works excluded from the
office of justifying by St. Paul are, characteristically and exclusively, " works done *before* the grace
of Christ and inspiration of His Spirit." If the
contrary opinion, then, is entertained, it is entertained in opposition to the views of Hooker and
Augustine; and the proof of it ought to be pro-
portionately laborious and conclusive. How, however, stands the fact? Of all the treatises which,
at various times, have been composed in advocacy
of that view of the doctrine of justification by faith,
which I presume to consider as erroneous, perhaps,
at present, the most popular and authoritative is
the work on Justification by Bishop O'Brien. By
the Bishop the subject has been frequently repre-
sented as exhausted, and the doctrine of justification by faith, according to his view of it, placed
upon a rock from which all the efforts of its oppo-
nents, it is affirmed, will never be able to dislodge
it. Will it, then, be believed that, in this celebrated work, there is no argumentative notice
whatsoever of the doctrine held by Hooker and
Augustine—held (I am bold to say) by every re-

spectable writer (sharing their opinions) on this subject? The corruptions of the doctrine of justification are, according to the Bishop [1], of three classes, turning on assigning a different signification from what the Bishop considers is the true one, either to the term "works," the term "faith," or the term "justification." In addressing himself, however, to the task of illustrating and exposing the first of these three classes of alleged corruptions, the Bishop confines himself altogether to a notion (attributed, he says, to Origen, but erroneously, as he discovers, in a note) that the works excluded from the office of justifying by St. Paul are ceremonial, and not moral works. This position he, of course, finds no difficulty in overthrowing; and, after doing so, he appears to suppose that his road is open and unopposed to the conclusion that, under the denomination of the "deeds of the law," all works whatsoever are excluded from the office of justifying by St. Paul. The question is disposed of without even the semblance of a reference to the only class of adverse statements on the point which it was of any practical importance to the purposes of his argument that he should successfully confute. He celebrates a triumph without even reconnoitring the enemy. He captures a solitary straggler, and concludes the campaign to have terminated gloriously. In one place, it is true, the Bishop

---

[1] Serm. v.

makes a passing allusion to those who "are able
to find that, when the Apostle says, 'We conclude
that a man is justified by faith without the deeds
of the law,' he means that a man is justified partly
by faith and partly by the deeds of the law [2]," and,
in another, he notices the view of Bishop Bull, that
justifying faith is inclusive of the works of Christian piety [3]. But in each instance the opinion is
cited as bearing its own refutation on the face of
it; and the work is actually carried to its close
without even an attempt having been made to
show the ground of argument to be erroneous
which we have seen to be taken by Hooker and
Augustine, and which is occupied notoriously by
Baxter and by Bull. My object, then, in the present paper, will be that of showing, in conformity
with the sentiments of the writers here alluded to,
that the works excluded from the office of justifying by St. Paul are the works which *precede* faith,
not the works which follow it and are effects of it.

Let it be observed, then, in proof of this position, in the first place, that the works thus excluded by the Apostle from the office of justifying, are "*the deeds of the law.*" "We conclude
that a man is justified by faith without the *deeds*
(ἔργων) of the law,"—an expression by which,
indeed, Bishop O'Brien appears to understand the
obedience or moral excellence which the law required (and *which is equally required by the Gospel*);

---

[2] Serm. iv.          [3] Note on p. 10.

but which really stands for this obedience *peculiarly considered as meriting eternal life, according to the terms and conditions of the Law of Moses.* The deeds of the law are the acts of an obedience to that law (considered as a covenant of works), the promise of which is—" The man that doeth these things shall live in them;"—the penalty— " Cursed is he that continueth not in all the things that are written in the book of the law to do them." The conclusion, then, of the Apostle is, that by the deeds of this law shall no flesh be justified—that the law requires an extent of obedience which no mere man has ever rendered, or will ever be capable of rendering, and requires, too, an obedience of this extent, as the indispensable condition of justification by its works; from all which it follows that a man is justified— if justified at all—" without the deeds of the law." He is justified under the provisions of some other covenant. He is thrown for his justification on the righteousness of another, as being legally and personally unrighteous in himself. The deeds of the law, then, excluded from the office of justifying by the Apostle in this passage, are not numerically those "good works" which the law and the Gospel equally require, but those works *specially considered as answering the requirements of the Law of Moses,* considered as capable of " putting away sin," and " enduring the severity of God's judgment;" considered as exonerating from the curse, thus ascertained as being justly due to him who continueth not in all the things which are written in the book of this law to do them, and in the place of it, entitling to the life which it secures, by promise, to a punctual and undeviating compliance with its precept. And if "the deeds of the law" are not an expression for good works, under *every* consideration of them, but *exclusively considered as meriting according to the terms of the covenant of works propounded in the Law of Moses;* then it is apparent, that there is not any thing in the conclusion that "a man is justified by faith without the deeds of the law," which is inconsistent with the doctrine that we are "justified by works and not by faith only," in the simplest and most natural sense of those expressions; for it may obviously be true, that a man is justified by faith, and not by a meritorious obedience to the Law of Moses, and true, at the same time, that, while justified by faith, he is justified also by the works, which are faith acting, and coming out in its results: and which justify, not as satisfying the conditions of a covenant of works, but as imputed for righteousness, under a covenant of grace.

I am not now affirming this to be the case. I am simply affirming that, supposing it alleged to be so, there is nothing to discredit such an allegation, in the doctrine of St. Paul, that "a man is justified by faith without the deeds of the law" —that "the deeds of the law," "without" which, according to St. Paul, a man is justified, are an obedience altogether distinct in its conditions from that of the "works" *by* which a man is justified according to St. James, and that there is, in consequence, no inconsistency, nor an approach to inconsistency, in believing, according to the statement of the one, that "a man is justified by faith without the deeds of the law," and according to the statement of the other (in the simplest and most natural sense of his expressions), that "by works a man is justified, and not by faith only." And thus, II., the works excluded from the office of justifying by St. Paul are *works to be performed by a man in his own strength.* "What shall we say, then, that Abraham, our father, *as pertaining to the flesh*, hath found?" To be "married" to the law, and to "be in the flesh," are, in Scripture, palpably convertible expressions. The two covenants are distinguished by the Apostle as the covenants of "the letter" and "the spirit"— the letter which "killeth," and the spirit which "giveth life;" the one "the ministration of death," because written and engraven on stones only, "ordained," indeed, "to life," but "found unto death," because "weak through *the flesh*,"— promising blessing to obedience, but not assisting and enabling to obey: the other, the ministration of righteousness, and, in *consequence of being so,* "the ministration of the Spirit." And thus the deeds of the law are not merely an obedience, performed under the condition of its *perfectly* meeting the requirements of the Law of Moses, but this obedience *performed* by the man in his *own strength*, and as developed out of the resources of *the flesh*. " The law is not made for a righteous man." It is imposed upon a fallen sinner, to show him the extent of his responsibilities and his need of a Saviour ; and instead of promising " grace to help in time of need," directs him rather to think of divine justice as *requiring previously to be satisfied, before the interferences of grace* ⁴ and mercy become possible, even as " the woman is bound by the law to her husband so long as he liveth ;" so that, " if while her husband liveth she be married to another man, she shall be called an adulteress." The law stands between the man who is "under the law," and the dispensation to him of God's mercy, as the living husband stands between his wife and the possibility of her marrying another man. And hence it follows, that the deeds of the law are an obedience *rendered to the law in our own strength.* The law, as a rule of life, may be of course obeyed, by divine aids ; but the law, as a covenant of works, reminds the sinner of the obedience for which he is responsible, and which God *requires* from him as the condition of His favour, in his fallen state. And thus, III., the works excluded from justifying by St. Paul, are *those works which are opposed to Divine Grace* (" If it be of grace, then it is no more of works "). And

⁴ Rom. vii.

how, then, can those works be included in this
number " with " which " the *grace of God* is ex-
ceeding abundant "—works of which it is alike
the privilege and duty of the person doing them
to say, " Not I, but the *grace* of God which was
with me," works, " unto " which he has been
" *created in Christ Jesus?* " And thus, lastly,
the works excluded from justifying by St. Paul,
are works which, supposing that they justified,
would give, in doing so, " *whereof to glory;*" and
is this the case with any works of which the
person doing them has cause to say, " Not I, but
the grace of God which was with me ;" " Not I,
but Christ that liveth in me ? " The Apostle, in
employing these expressions, in effect denies the
works which a man does, with the aids of Divine
grace, to stand on the same ground as those which
he has performed in his own strength. He affirms,
in effect, that while a man would have " whereof
to glory," in performance of the one, it is not, on
the contrary, he, but Divine grace which carries
away the entire glory of the other. On the whole,
then, it is untrue that the works excluded from
justifying by St. Paul are identical with those
" by " which " a man is justified," according to
St. James. The works, on the contrary, excluded
from justifying by St. Paul, are precisely those
which have been done, as Hooker and Augustine
tell us, " *before* the grace of Christ and inspiration
of His Spirit." He excludes no others, *not* because the justifying efficacy which he denies to

" works done before the grace of Christ," is *attri-butable* to the works which are done *after* it, *but because* no other works *but those* of which he speaks, under the denomination of " the deeds of the law," could make *their* pretensions to confer the *legal* righteousness of which he is here speaking. It never entered into the mind of the Apostle to explain that the works of an evangelical obedience were unequal to the office of investing with a legal righteousness, unequal to the office of " putting away sin," or " enduring the severity of God's judgment." It is obviously impossible that any acts should have a moral value higher than, or distinct from, the principles they flow from. And what is it, accordingly, to be justified by the works, which are faith acting, but to be " justified by faith ;" as what is it to be justified by faith, but to be " accepted in the Beloved," in *the view of us, as confiding in Him*—that is, expecting our happiness, for time and for eternity, *from the fulfilment of His promises, and, accordingly, in the way of His obedience ?*

CATHOLICUS.

# LETTER III.

Sir,

Much reliance appears to be placed by solifidian writers on two collateral arguments in favour
of their scheme, which I think that it may be
useful distinctly to consider. One of these is a
doctrinal, the other a practical argument—one
founded on the interpretation of Scripture, the
other on the practical effects as illustrated in indi-
viduals.

I. First, then, it is affirmed that the possible
misapplication of his doctrine, contemplated by
St. Paul, when he proposed the question, "What
shall we say, then; shall we continue in sin that
grace may abound[1]?" is proof that the Pauline
doctrine of justification is not that of justification
by works, or moral obedience, inasmuch as who
would think of taking encouragement for con-
tinuing in sin, from a doctrine of justification
which formally suspended the benefit on the con-

[1] Rom. vi. 1.

dition of penitence and new obedience? And
hence (it is said) the inevitable inference, that the
benefit of justification is suspended by St. Paul on
no condition of the kind; that justification (according to the doctrine of St. Paul) is by faith,
and by faith only, without the concurrence of any
description of good works—a doctrine which has
always been loaded with the opprobrium of licen-
tiousness, which has some appearance (at least, on
the first blush) of vacating the necessity for obedience and good works, but which, instead of
being liable to objection from this circumstance,
derives from it, on the contrary, the final and
indispensable evidence of its identity with the
doctrine of St. Paul. Such is the manner in which
solifidian writers argue from the question proposed
by the Apostle at the opening of the sixth chapter
of the Romans, " What shall we say, then; shall
we continue in sin that grace may abound?"
" How " the Apostle " answers this question,"
Bishop O'Brien says that " it is beside " his " purpose to notice *." The fact, however, is, that the
Apostle's answer to the question is destructive
of the argument thus built upon it. It is, in
effect, that his doctrine of justification *precludes
the very notion of the justified man's continuance* in
sin—that " a death unto sin and a new birth unto
righteousness " is the very grace which faith receives, and which baptism administers. " *How*

* P. 101.

shall we, who are dead to sin, live any longer therein?" while, further on, (ver. 16,) he affirms in terms, that "righteousness" is suspended on the condition of "obedience," and that death is the judicially inevitable consequence of unrepented "sin." So premature is the solifidian conclusion from the question, "Shall we continue in sin that grace may abound?" The Apostle's own reply to the inquiry is to the effect, that, suspended on the condition of penitence and new obedience, it is impossible that the justification of the Christian should consist with a continuance in sin. But then, the question itself!—Surely it implies that there was something in the doctrine of justification (as the Apostle had been previously propounding it) to give rise to this idea. Undoubtedly there was. And it is evident, also, what this was. The Apostle, up to the end of the fifth chapter, had been occupied in asserting the doctrine of justification by grace through faith, as opposed to the doctrine of justification by the deeds of the law, and he had just remarked that it was so far from being the case, that "the law was given" that "righteousness should be" by "it, that it actually" entered, "that the offence might abound," and by abounding, illustrate all the more conspicuously, the riches of that grace which abounded, notwithstanding, even more. After this, then, it was no impertinent or unnatural inquiry, whether we should not continue in sin that grace might abound, whether, if it was (as St. Paul had stated

it to be) the case, that the aboundings of man's sin
were the very means of bringing into manifestation, and so of glorifying, the *super*-aboundings of
God's grace,] it did not follow, according to this
statement, that the way to glorify God was to
continue in sin, in order to give all the greater
occasion for the exercise and manifestation of His
grace.   This, I conceive, is the obvious and sufficient account of the inquiry with which the sixth
chapter of the Epistle to the Romans opens—not
that the *entire* doctrine of justification, as propounded by St. Paul in this Epistle, was exposed
to a construction like the one implied in the terms
of this inquiry, but that such a question arose
naturally *at that point* of his argument at which
the Apostle had arrived at the *close of the fifth*
chapter—that it was suggested by the doctrine of
justification by grace through faith, as St. Paul
had been *hitherto* asserting it—that is, as opposed
to the doctrine of justification by the deeds of the
law—calling accordingly (for the sake of obviating
the notion that the Apostle's doctrine was in
reality exposed to any such construction) for that
explanation of the *plan* and *method* of God's grace
as proposed to us in the Gospel, which the Apostle
immediately proceeds to give, and which occupies
him throughout the sixth, seventh, and eighth
chapters.   The Apostle had propounded but *half*
his doctrine of justification up to the close of the
fifth chapter; the sixth, seventh, and eighth chapters are devoted to the exposition of the *other half*.

He had exhibited, *principally, one phase* of it in
the class of statements with which he had been
dealing in the earlier chapters. He goes on, in
this, to the exhibition of its *other phase.* He had
asserted already the doctrine of justification by
grace through faith, in opposition to the doctrine of
justification by a meritorious obedience to the law
of Moses. He now asserts the doctrine of justification by a grace which suspends on the condition
of "a death unto sin and a new birth unto righteousness," the justification which it offers—working
itself, indeed, this "death unto sin and new birth
unto righteousness," in as many as believe, and
laying it, at the same time, at the foundation of
all hope of pardoning mercy, and divine acceptance—the salvation, doubtless, by grace through
faith, but the *object* of faith, a Saviour associating
sinners in His life, and conforming them to His
image, and the *act* of faith accordingly, the act of
expecting pardon through His blood, on the condition of welcoming His Spirit and minding His
directions. Such, I conceive, is the account to be
afforded of St. Paul's inquiry, "Shall we continue
in sin that grace may abound?" in connexion
with the answer which he gives to it; an account
of it which rescues the scriptural doctrine of justification from an exception of some speciousness,
and shows that there is nothing whatsoever to
embarrass the doctrine of justification by conditional works in the terms of this inquiry.

II. Another objection to the doctrine of justifica-

tion by conditional works, is drawn from the
practical tendency and consequences of this doctrine. Of its inconsistency with "peace and joy
in believing" the experience and testimony of
Dr. Johnson in particular, (O'Brien, p. 332[3],) is
adduced as satisfactory and conclusive evidence.
Dr. Johnson (Boswell, a Day at Dilley's,) asserts
that "no rational man can die without uneasy
apprehensions," because "no man can be sure
that his repentance and obedience will obtain salvation;" and hence (it is argued) the inconsistency
with peace of the doctrine of salvation by conditional works. May it not, however, be inquired,
why so much reliance is reposed in a question of
this kind, on the authority of Dr. Johnson? Why
the testimony of a "moralist" is adduced instead

---

[3] The discrepancy of sentiment on a cardinal point between the
two most celebrated of our more recent solifidian writers is re-
markable. Bishop O'Brien, in the note to which I am referring,
characterizes as "new in Protestant theology," and "most strange,"
Bishop Bull's remark : " 'resipiscentiam non esse opus unicum
aut simplex sed multorum aliorum operum quasi complexionem ;'
these ' opera pœnitentiæ ' being (according to Bishop Bull's enume-
ration) *eleven* in number. On the contrary, according to Professor
Garbett, (Bampton Lecture, iv. p. 395,) not only in the internal
workings of repentance are there many acts, but in the preparatory
condition of repentance there are many acts, which, as previous
conditions, are indispensable. They are a sine quâ non. *No
judicious advocate of* justification by faith only *means to dispute*
this. So that if there were one hundred works, instead of the ten
or twelve which Bull enumerates, the case is not altered." Can
Bishop O'Brien and Mr. Garbett be advocating one and the *same*
doctrine of Justification?

of that of a divine,—why the views and experience of a man eminent only for the "wisdom of this world," are made to stand as criteria of a doctrine at once held and advocated by Baxter, by Doddridge, by Davenant, and by Bull? Surely if the experience of these eminent men directly contradicts the sentiment that "no rational man can die without uneasy apprehensions" as long as he considers his salvation as suspended on the condition of good works, in this case, one or other of these two conclusions would appear to be inevitable: either, first, that the doctrine held by Dr. Johnson at the time is less inconsistent with "peace and joy in believing," than he considered it to be; or else, (which I apprehend to be the true account of the difference,) that the doctrine of conditional works, as held by these divines, is one essentially different, and easily distinguishable, from the legal and depressing views of Dr. Johnson. It is true, indeed, that as Dr. Johnson held that no man speaking "the words of truth and soberness," would ever say that he was "sure of his salvation," so these writers (as the result of personal experience gained perhaps among some of the holiest people of their day) declare it to have been a "very small number that they could ever hear say, I ·am sure of my justification and salvation[4]," and that "the generality of Christians are exercised with many doubts about

---

[4] Cath. Theol. of God's Gov., sect. 16.

their own state[5]," and that thus "the cer-
tainty of salvation is very rare;" but then we
hear from the same writers of "a great number who have lived in holy confidence, hope,
and peace, and some in great joy, but most in
*tolerable* fears and doubting, and *some few op-
pressed* by those doubts;" and that thus, "where
there is not full assurance, there may neverthe-
less" (instead of the "uneasy apprehension" so
inevitable in the view of Dr. Johnson) "be a
cheerful and prevailing hope[6];" and this, also,
for an obvious reason, namely, that according to
the views of these divines, the hope of the Christian springs from the sincerity, not from the mea-
sure and amount of his obedience, from his expe-
rienced and proved spirituality of principle and
aim, and not from the degree of his attainments;
from his works, considered, not as the meritorious
fulfilment of a legal condition, but as the opera-
tion, and accordingly as the evidence, of an evangelical and lively faith.   There is surely all the
difference in the world between the theology of a
person looking to his "obedience and repentance"
to "obtain salvation" in the former sense, and
that of a person thinking of them as the conditions on which salvation is suspended in the latter.
I may feel, for instance, and see by its results,
that my repentance and obedience is sincere and
real; and I may feel at the same moment, and

---

[5] Doddridge, Lectures on the Doctrine of Assurance.
[6] Cath. Theol. and Doddridge's Lectures, as above.

discern by the results, that it is defective and contaminated. Let me think, then, that God demands from me, as the condition of His favour and forgiveness, an exercise of repentance and obedience in the full (or any thing approaching to the full) extent of my responsibilities, and I "must be contented to acknowledge that death is a terrible thing to my life's end." Let me have reason for believing, on the contrary, that the condition on which salvation is suspended is that of a sincere and real, though, to the last, defective repentance and obedience, and in this case the very same repentance and obedience (which, supposing it regarded in the light of a meritorious fulfilment of condition, would have plunged me in despondency, if it did not in despair,) considered now as simply evidential of a lively faith, as, indeed, a sine quâ non in respect of its existence, but not in respect of its perfection, considered as the vital action of the new creation in Christ Jesus,) becomes, however feeble or however sickly, the source of an encouragement and hope which is lively and prevailing in proportion to the conviction which I feel, not of its perfection of degree, but of its reality and truth. And the simple question then is, whether a man can ever be "assured," or ever reach with reason a "cheerful and prevailing hope," that his repentance and obedience are sincere and spiritual. If he can, then the doctrine of salvation by conditional works, in the sense in which it is maintained by Bull and Davenant, by

Baxter and Doddridge, may consist with "peace and joy in believing and abounding hope'." If it cannot, no *sufficient* foundation for this peace and joy is laid, in this case, even in *the doctrine of justification by faith only*, inasmuch as if we are incapable of knowing that our repentance is sincere, we *must be equally incapable of ascertaining the liveliness of our faith.* If we can tell that our hearts are changed, we may then tell that our repentance is sincere; and if we cannot, it is in vain in this case to suppose that we can ever have the comfort of finding our faith lively. It appears, then, to be a groundless imputation on the doctrine of salvation by conditional works, as affirmed by our divines, that it militates with the peace and hope which so characteristically belong to the true members of Christ's body. The doctrine, on the contrary, has been affirmed from the earliest pe-

---

⁷ It may, possibly, be as well to cite the doctrine of Doddridge on this subject. It is that "faith in Christ is in general committing our souls to Him for salvation in His appointed way." Lectures, Part v. Defin. 82. It "includes in its nature and inseparable effects the whole of moral virtue. (Corollary 1, on the same.) Some divines have chosen to call this purpose of holy obedience essential to true faith *internal* good works, and the fruit actually produced in this life *external;* and in this sense it must be acknowledged that, according to our definition of faith . . . we maintain the universal necessity of good works as much as any can do. (Scholium 2 on Corollary 2.) All those passages which declare holiness to be necessary to salvation would be utterly inconsistent with the promises made to faith, (see O'Brien, Serm. vi. p. 146,) if faith did not imply such a prevailing resolution of holy obedience." (Propos. 137, Dem. vol. ii. p. 231.)

riod of the Christian era to the present moment, by the holiest, the happiest, and most discriminating of all Christians. It was (according to Milner, and "his witness is true") the doctrine of the entire army of the Church's martyrs, in the primitive ages of the Gospel. It was the doctrine of St. Augustine when raised up to invigorate and elevate her piety in the fifth century, and (amidst all the disturbing influences by which it has been encountered since the days of Luther) it has still remained the doctrine of the best and wisest of our theologians of all denominations, and all times, of Bull and Davenant, of Baxter and of Doddridge. In fine, then, in the words of Baxter [s], "the great justification by faith, mentioned so oft in Scripture, is, upon merely believing we are first made just by free-given pardon, and right to life (and true sanctification with it), and we are sentenced just, because so first made just. But this is not without our faith and repentance. 2ndly, And that faith and repentance are a righteousness evangelical, i. e. a performance of the condition on which the covenant of grace doth freely give us right to Christ, pardon and life, and so are the constitutive causes of the subordinate justification.

" *Objection.*—By this you will fall in with the Papists, who take justification partly by Christ's righteousness, and partly by our own, and partly in pardon, and partly in faith and holiness.

[s] Cath. Theol. b. 2, Eleventh Day's Conference.

" *Answer.*—Tell not me of the names of Papists or any to frighten me from plain Scripture truth. Why may not I rather say—why do you go from all the ancient writers and Churches, even Augustine himself, by your new and contrary opinion? Was true justification unknown for so many hundred years after the Apostles? What an honour is done to Popery, and what a dishonour to the reformed Churches, when it shall be concluded that all the Churches heretofore, even next after the age of the Apostles, and almost all the present Churches, were, and are, against the doctrine of the Protestants, and on the Papists' side. And yet how many do us this injury, and the Roman Church this honour. About the nature of justifying faith, and its office to justification, and about the nature of justification itself, and imputation of righteousness, and free-will, and about man's works and merits, and about assurance of salvation and perseverance, how many do call that Popery which the whole current of Greek and Latin Fathers do assert, and all the ancient Churches owned, and most of all the present Churches in the world [9]."

CATHOLICUS.

[9] Thirteenth Day's Conference. " Error, Sin, and Danger which many fall into on Pretence of avoiding Popery."

# POSTSCRIPT, 1862.

---

IT would be easy to fortify the view of justification taken in these letters, with many additional authorities, as of Bp. Hall, who says [1] : " God doth not justify the wicked man *as such;* but, of wicked, makes him good; not by a mere acceptation, but by a real change, while He justifies those whom He sanctifies." And of Bp. Davenant, one of whose propositions in his Treatise on Justification [2] is: " Some good works are necessary to justification, as concurrent or preliminary conditions, although they are not necessary, as efficient or meritorious causes." It has been my wish, however, to make this discussion as brief as the object which it contemplates would conveniently admit; and I shall, therefore, terminate it at this point with a single remark. It is this,— Would the reader bring his scheme of justification to a safe test, let him try it by the relation in

---

[1] Old Religion.     [2] CXXXI. Allport's Translation.

which it stands to the doctrine of the Redeemer's Intercession,—a doctrine denounced by Mr. Maurice[3], and without a place in that system of theology of which, after a lapse of thirty years, Bishop O'Brien appears before the public, in a second edition, as the deliberate and persevering advocate. Of the theologians of this school, it is the remark of Baxter[4], and the same remark is made, in substance, by Dean Jackson[5], that " they look on Christ Himself as if they had no more use for Him, either to continue their justification or forgive their sin," —a remark the truth of which is confirmed both by Owen[6] and Goodwin[7], each of whom complains of the *neglect* of the doctrine of the Redeemer's intercession by the Christians of their day,—the disciples, in effect, truer than their masters to the tendencies and instincts of the theology in which they had been educated. And this, indeed, is the way always. The Romanism with which we are popularly and practically conversant is not exactly the Romanism of the decrees of the Council of Trent, and in Protestant Schools similarly, the error which exists in a form of mitigation, and lies half concealed in the writings of the learned though mistaken theo-

---

[3] On Sacrifice, p. 259.  Compare Rom. v. 8—11.
[4] Life of Faith, c. vii.
[5] B. x.
[6] On Hebrews vii. 25.
[7] On Election, b. iv. c. 8.

logian, displays its virus mainly in that popular
theology which is the mischievous, but legitimate
and inevitable application of his doctrines. Thus
an erroneous system of theology, like " evil men,"
" will wax worse and worse." The happy inconsistency which their learning and fidelity to Scripture impose on its first authors, or more learned
advocates, is remarked by the common run of
their disciples, not as inspiring any doubt about
the soundness of the theology itself, but as a
reason for carrying out its principles into the
application, which they see that they require,
though an application monstrous in itself, and in
the flattest contradiction to the Word of God.
And hence that " progress of error " of which the
history of the Church supplies us with so many
conspicuous examples. " It is *sensible* to think,"
says Lord Bacon [8], " that when men enter first
into search and inquiry, according to the social
frames and compositions of their understanding,
they light on different conceits, and so all opinions
and doubts are beaten over, and then men having
made a taste of all, wax weary of variety, and so
reject the worst and hold themselves to the best ·
. . . . . which, afterwards, are received and carried on, and the rest extinct. *But* Truth is contrary, and Time is like a river which carrieth
down things which are light and blown up, and

[8] Of the Interpretation of Nature, c. 7.

sinketh and drowneth that which is sad and weighty. For, the state of knowledge is ever a democracy, and that prevaileth which is most agreeable to the senses and conceits of people."

THE END.

GILBERT AND RIVINGTON, PRINTERS, ST. JOHN'S SQUARE, LONDON.

# 𝔑𝔢𝔴 𝔚𝔬𝔯𝔨𝔰 𝔞𝔫𝔡 𝔑𝔢𝔴 𝔈𝔡𝔦𝔱𝔦𝔬𝔫𝔰,

PUBLISHED BY

## MESSRS. RIVINGTON,

3, WATERLOO PLACE, PALL MALL, LONDON.

---

Eighteen Years of a Clerical Meeting;
being the Minutes of the Alcester Clerical Association
from June, 1842, to August, 1860;
with a Preface on the Revival of Ruri-Decanal Chapters.
Edited by RICHARD SEYMOUR, M.A.,
Rector of Kinwarton, and Rural Dean; and
JOHN F. MACKARNESS, M.A.,
late Vicar of Tardebigge, in the Diocese of Worcester,
now Rector of Honiton.
In one Volume, crown 8vo. 6s. 6d. (*Now ready.*)

" If these records have any merit, it is that they contain a history of
clerical opinion during a not uneventful period, and a proof that the
internal conflict of theological parties in the Church, often assumed to
be more bitter than it really is, may easily be tempered by good sense
and practical wisdom into friendly and not unprofitable discussion."
*Extract from Preface.*

---

Thoughts on Personal Religion.
By EDWARD MEYRICK GOULBURN, D.D.,
Prebendary of St. Paul's, and one of Her
Majesty's Chaplains in Ordinary.
In two Volumes, small 8vo. 10s. 6d. (*Just published.*)

## The Man Christ Jesus ; or, the Daily Life
### and Teaching of Our Lord, in Childhood and Manhood, on Earth.

By the Rev. THOMAS MARKBY, M.A.,
Sometime Afternoon Preacher at St. James's,
Paddington.

Crown 8vo.   9s. 6d.   (*Lately published.*)

———•———

## Praise, Precept, and Prayer;
### a Complete Manual of Family Worship.

### By JOHN M. CLABON.

Part I. : Selections from the Old Testament, principally
of Praise, for Morning Use.

Part II.: Selections from the Old and New Testaments,
and from the best Commentators, for Evening
Use.

Part III.: Selections from "The Imitation of Christ."

Part IV.: Prayers for Six Weeks.           .

The Editor has endeavoured to extract all that is
most beautiful and most useful from the Bible, and
from the writings of the great men who have made
it their special study.

In one Vol., 8vo. (pp. 650), price 16s.

(*Lately published.*)

———•— ‑‑

RIVINGTONS, WATERLOO PLACE, LONDON.

## Ordination Lectures,

delivered in Riseholme Palace Chapel, during
Ember Weeks.

By the Rev. HENRY MACKENZIE, M.A.,

One of the Chaplains to the Lord Bishop of Lincoln,
&c. &c.

CONTENTS:—Pastoral Government—Educational Work
—Self-government in the Pastor—Missions and their
Reflex Results — Dissent — Public Teaching — Sunday
Schools—Doctrinal Controversy—Secular Aids.

Small 8vo. 3*s*. (*Now ready.*)

―――

## The Beginning of the Book of Genesis,

with Notes and Reflections.

By the Rev. ISAAC WILLIAMS, B.D.

Printed uniformly with Mr. WILLIAMS's Harmony and
Commentary on the Gospels, in small 8vo. 7*s*. 6*d*.

(*Just published.*)

―――

RIVINGTONS, WATERLOO PLACE, LONDON.

## The Holy Year ;
### or, Hymns for Sundays and Holy Days, and for other Occasions.

Small 8vo.   4s. 6d.   (*Just published.*)

---

## The Limits of Religious Belief:
### Suggestions addressed to the Student in Divine Things.

By the Rev. WM. BENTINCK HAWKINS,
M.A., F.R.S.,
of Exeter College, Oxford.

Small 8vo.   2s. 6d.   (*Just published.*)

---

## Recent Recollections of the Anglo-American Church in the United States.

By an English Layman, five years resident in that Republic.

In 2 vols. post 8vo.   18s.

---

RIVINGTONS, WATERLOO PLACE, LONDON.

Sermons on Various Subjects and Occasions.
By EDWARD MEYRICK GOULBURN, D.D.
In two Volumes, small 8vo., uniform with "Thoughts on
Personal Religion." (*In the Press.*)

————

The Greek Testament ; with a critically -
revised Text: a Digest of Various Readings :
Marginal References to Verbal and Idiomatic Usage :
Prolegomena : and a copious Critical and Exegetical
Commentary in English.
For the Use of Theological Students and Ministers.

By HENRY ALFORD, D.D.,
Dean of Canterbury.

Now complete, in 4 Vols. or 5 Parts, 8vo., price £5 2*s*.

Or separately as follows :—

Vol. I.—THE FOUR GOSPELS. *Fourth Edition.* 28*s*.

Vol. II.—ACTS to II. CORINTHIANS. *Fourth Edit.* 24*s*.

Vol. III.—GALATIANS to PHILEMON. *Third Edition.*
18*s*.

Vol. IV., Part I.—HEBREWS to II. PETER. *Second
Edition.* 18*s*.

Vol. IV., Part II.—I. JOHN to REVELATION. *Second
Edition.* 14*s*.

————

RIVINGTONS, WATERLOO PLACE, LONDON.

## The Unsealed Visions of Daniel;
Their Age, their Authenticity, and their Fulfilment.
With a Rectification of Ancient Chronology,
adjusting it to the Christian Æra.
### By W. R. A. BOYLE.
In one Volume, 8vo.   (*In the Press.*)

———◆———

## Holy Day and Occasional Sermons,
Preached in the Parish Church of St. Mary the Virgin,
Dover.
### By the Rev. JOHN PUCKLE, M.A.,
Vicar of the Parish, and Rural Dean.
8vo.   9*s.*

———◆———

## The Sea-board and the Down; or, My Parish
in the South.
### By JOHN WOOD WARTER, B.D.,
Vicar of West Tarring, Sussex.
In 2 vols. small 4to., with Illustrations.   28*s.*

———◆———

RIVINGTONS, WATERLOO PLACE, LONDON.

The New Testament of our Lord and Saviour
Jesus Christ, in the original Greek.
With Notes and Introductions.
By CHR. WORDSWORTH, D.D.,
Canon of Westminster.

In Four Parts or Two Vols., imperial 8vo., 4*l.* 4*s.*

*Separately,*

Part I.: The Four Gospels. *Second Edition.* 1*l.* 1*s.*
Part II.: The Acts. *Second Edition.* 10*s.* 6*d.*
Part III.: The Epistles of St. Paul. *Second Edition.*
1*l.* 11*s.* 6*d.*
Part IV.: The General Epistles and Book of Revelation.
1*l.* 1*s.*

— ◆ —

De Viris Illustribus Urbis Romæ, a Romulo ad
Augustum. An Elementary Latin Reading Book,
being a Series of Biographical Chapters
on Roman History, chronologically arranged;
*simplified* from the Text of Livy and other Roman writers;
adapted, with Annotations and a Vocabulary, from the
work of Professor Lhomond.

By the Editor of the " Graduated Series of English
Reading Books."
Small 8vo. 3*s.*

— ◆ —

RIVINGTONS, WATERLOO PLACE, LONDON.

# The Inspiration of the Bible:
Five Lectures, delivered in Westminster Abbey.
By CHRISTOPHER WORDSWORTH, D.D., Canon
of Westminster.

Post 8vo. 3s. 6d.

———•———

# The Interpretation of the Bible:
Five Lectures, delivered in Westminster Abbey.

By the same Author.

Post 8vo. 3s. 6d.

———•———

# Notes on the Epistle to the Hebrews,
with Analysis and Brief Paraphrase. For Theological
Students.

By the Rev. E. H. KNOWLES,
late Michel Fellow of Queen's College, Oxford.

Dedicated by permission to the Lord Bishop of Oxford.

Crown 8vo. 6s. 6d.

———•———

RIVINGTONS, WATERLOO PLACE, LONDON.

## Parochial Sermons;

By the Rev. J. K. MILLER,
late Vicar of Walkeringham, Notts, and formerly
Fellow of Trinity College, Cambridge.

Small 8vo. 4s. 6d.

---

## Meditations for a Month, on Select Passages
### of Scripture.

By CHARLOTTE AUGUSTA SNEYD.

Small 8vo. 3s. 6d.

---

## Parish Musings; or, Devotional Poems.

By JOHN S. B. MONSELL, LL.D.,
Vicar of Egham, Surrey, and Rural Dean.

*Fifth Edition.* 2s.

---

RIVINGTONS, WATERLOO PLACE, LONDON.

# England, the Remnant of Judah, and the Israel of Ephraim.
## By the Rev. F. R. A. GLOVER, M.A.,
Chaplain to the Consulate at Cologne.

In 8vo. 6s. 6d.

———

# The Revelation of Jesus Christ ;
Expounded by FRANCIS BODFIELD HOOPER,
Rector of Upton Warren, Worcestershire,
Author of " A Guide to the Apocalypse," and other
Works.

In 2 vols. 8vo. 28s.

———

Village Sermons, preached at some of the
chief Christian Seasons, in the Parish Church
of Belleau with Aby.

*other of*

*J. A. Giles*

*wla tor of Bede &*

By J. D. GILES, M.A.,
late Rector.

Small 8vo. 5s.

———

RIVINGTONS, WATERLOO PLACE, LONDON.

## Miscellaneous Sermons preached at St. Mary's Church, Marylebone.

### By JOHN HAMPDEN GURNEY, M.A.

In small 8vo. 6s.

By the same Author,

Sermons on Old Testament Histories. *Second Edition.* 6s.

Sermons on Texts from the Epistles and Gospels. *Second Edition.* 6s.

---

## The Old Man's Rambles.

New and Cheaper Edition. 3s. 6d.

---

## The Way of Holiness in Married Life.

A Course of Sermons preached in Lent.

### By HENRY J. ELLISON, M.A.,

Vicar of Windsor, Prebendary of Lichfield, and Reader to the Queen at Windsor Castle.

*New and cheaper Edition.* In small 8vo. 2s. 6d.

---

RIVINGTONS, WATERLOO PLACE, LONDON.

## Contributions to an Amateur Magazine
in Prose and Verse.

### By RICHARD PERRY, M.A.,
formerly Scholar of Trinity College, Cambridge.

Second Edition, with Additions.   In crown 8vo.   8s. 6d.

---

## The Prayer of Prayers.

By the Hon. and Rev. ROBERT HENLEY, M.A.,
Perpetual Curate of Putney.

Small 8vo.   4s. 6d.

---

## Sermons for Households,

By FRANCIS E. C. BYNG, M.A.,
Rector of Little Casterton.

Crown 8vo.   3s. 6d.

---

RIVINGTONS, WATERLOO PLACE, LONDON.

Lectures, Historical, Doctrinal, and Practical, on the Catechism of the Church of England.

By FRANCIS-RUSSELL NIXON, D.D.,
Lord Bishop of Tasmania.

*Sixth Edition.* 8vo. 18*s.*

———

Ezekiel's Sign, Metrically Paraphrased and Interpreted, from his Fourth and Fifth Chapters ; with Notes and Elucidations from the Sculptured Slabs of Nineveh.

By W. B. GALLOWAY, M.A.,
Incumbent of St. Mark's, Regent's Park, and Chaplain to the Viscount Hawarden.

Small 8vo. 2*s.* 6*d.*

———

Bible Servants, and what they Teach us.
By the Rev. JOHN D. LETTS, M.A., Domestic Chaplain to the Earl Ferrers.

18mo., with Frontispiece. 3*s.*

———

RIVINGTONS, WATERLOO PLACE, LONDON.

# The Gospel Narrative of our Lord's Passion
## harmonized, with Reflections.
### By the Rev. ISAAC WILLIAMS, B.D.,
### late Fellow of Trinity College, Oxford.

*Fifth Edition.*  8s.

\*\*\* This is one Volume of a Harmony and Commentary on the whole Gospel Narrative, by the same Author, in 8 vols., small 8vo., price 3l. 6s.   They are sold separately as follows—

1. Thoughts on the Study of the Gospels, 8s.

2. Harmony of the Evangelists, 8s. 6d.

3. The Nativity (extending to the Calling of St. Matthew), 8s. 6d.

4. Second Year of the Ministry, 8s.

5. Third Year of the Ministry, 8s. 6d.

6. The Holy Week, 8s. 6d.        7. The Passion, 8s.

8. The Resurrection, 8s.

---

# New and cheaper Editions of Cotterill's
## Selection of Psalms and Hymns for Public Worship.

### In 32mo., 1s.; in 18mo. (large print), 1s. 6d.
### Also an Edition on fine paper, 2s. 6d.

\*\*\* A large allowance to Clergymen and Churchwardens.

---

RIVINGTONS, WATERLOO PLACE, LONDON.

The SEVENTH EDITION of A PRACTICAL INTRODUCTION to GREEK ACCIDENCE; with Easy Exercises and Vocabulary. By the same Author. 5s. 6d.

The SECOND EDITION of the ORATION of DEMOSTHENES on the CROWN, edited, from the best Text, with ENGLISH NOTES, and Grammatical References. By the same. 4s. 6d.

The SECOND EDITION of the PHILIPPIC ORATIONS of DEMOS-THENES, with ENGLISH NOTES. By the same. 4s.

The SECOND EDITION of SPELLING TURNED ETYMOLOGY, PART I. By the same Author. 2s. 6d.

The SIXTH EDITION of an ENGLISH GRAMMAR for CLASSICAL SCHOOLS; being a Practical Introduction to ENGLISH PROSE COMPOSITION, with Syntax and Exercises. By the same. 4s. 6d.

A NEW EDITION of ELEMENTS of INSTRUCTION on the CHURCH. For the use of Schools. By CHR. WORDSWORTH, D.D., Canon of Westminster. 18mo. 2s.

---

*Messrs.* RIVINGTON'S *Classified School Catalogue may be had gratis on application.*

---

RIVINGTONS, WATERLOO PLACE, LONDON.